FAVOURITE
PIES &
TARTS

*with illustrations of
cottage life by
Henry Edward Spernon T*

Index

Cover pictures *front:* "Preparing the Meal'
back: "The Evening Meal"
Title page: "Reading the News"

Printed and Published by J. Salmon Ltd., Sevenoaks, England © Copyright

Country Pork Pie

Ideal for a buffet or summer picnic. Serve with English mustard and a mixed salad.

18 oz. shortcrust pastry	2 tbsp. Worcestershire Sauce
6 oz. bacon, rinds removed, minced	1 teaspoon dried sage
1½ lb. lean minced pork	Salt & freshly ground black pepper
1 onion, skinned and chopped	4 hard-boiled eggs
12 oz. pork sausagemeat	Beaten egg for glazing

Set oven to 400°F or Mark 6. Roll out two thirds of the pastry and use to line a greased 8 inch circular loose-bottomed cake tin. Mix together remaining ingredients except for the eggs. Place half of this mixture in the lined tin, place the eggs on top and cover with the rest of the pork mixture. Roll out the rest of the pastry to make a lid. Moisten the edges of the pastry, cover with the lid and seal the edges well. Trim off any excess pastry and make a slit in the centre. Decorate the top with any remaining pastry. Glaze with the beaten egg. Bake in the oven for 1½ hours, covering the top with foil after half an hour to avoid excess browning. Allow to cool in the tin before removing. Serves 8-10.

Vegetable Tart

The breadcrumb topping gives a slightly crunchy texture to this tart.

7 oz. flour   4 oz. butter   Salt & pepper   1 medium onion, chopped
2 oz. button mushrooms, sliced thinly   8 fl.oz. milk   4 oz. Cheddar, grated
2 eggs, separated   1 lb. cauliflower florets cooked until just soft
2 tablespoons dried breadcrumbs

Set oven to 400°F or Mark 6. In a bowl, rub 3 oz. butter into 6 oz. flour. Add approx. 2 tablespoons of cold water to bind together into a short dough. Roll out and use to line a greased 10 inch flan tin. Using a fork, prick pastry case all over, line with greaseproof paper and cover with baking beans. Bake blind for approximately 30 minutes or until pastry is cooked, removing beans and greaseproof paper after 15 minutes. In a small saucepan melt rest of the butter, add onion and mushrooms and stir over a medium heat until onion is soft and mushrooms are well cooked. Add remaining flour, stirring well. Slowly mix in milk, bringing to the boil, stirring continuously until thickened. Stir in cheese and season with salt and pepper. Remove from heat and beat in egg yolks. Whisk the egg whites separately and fold into the sauce. Arrange cauliflower over base of the pastry, spoon over the sauce and sprinkle with breadcrumbs. Bake for 15 minutes until base has set and is browned. Serve immediately. Serves 6-8.

Steak and Kidney Pie

*A distinctive British dish, often made as a one-crust pie, where the
filling is covered but not completely enclosed by the pastry.*

**1 oz. flour   Salt and pepper   1½ lb. stewing steak cubed
6 oz. ox kidney, cores removed and cubed   1 oz. butter
1 large onion peeled and chopped   ¼ pint beef stock   ¼ pint brown ale
1 bayleaf   1 tablespoon Worcestershire sauce
1 tablespoon tomato purée   9 oz. shortcrust pastry   Beaten egg for glazing**

Season flour with salt and pepper. Roll meat in flour and shake well. Reserve
remaining flour. Melt butter in a large pan, add chopped onion and cook for
3 minutes stirring occasionally. Increase heat add meat and seal. Add
remaining flour and cook for 2-3 minutes, stirring frequently. Add bayleaf,
Worcestershire sauce, tomato purée, then slowly pour in stock and ale, bring to
the boil stirring constantly. Cover, reduce heat to a bare simmer and cook for
1½-2 hours. Set oven to 400°F or Mark 6. Transfer cooked meat to a 3 pint pie
dish. Roll out pastry so that it is 2 inches larger than the dish and cut off a ½
inch strip from around the outside. Dampen the edge of the pie dish and place
strip around the lip. Moisten pastry strip and cover the pie with remaining
pastry lid. Ensuring edges are sealed, knock back and trim off excess. Shape
trimmings and use to decorate top of pie. Brush with beaten egg to glaze and
cook for 35-40 minutes in oven. Serves 4.

Stilton and Walnut Pie

This tasty pie is best eaten when just warm or completely cold, served with a salad.

**12 oz. flour   8 oz. chilled salted butter   12 oz. full fat cream cheese
2 medium eggs   2 tablespoons parsley sprigs   6 oz. stilton, grated
6 oz. walnuts, chopped   1 large onion peeled and chopped
1 tablespoon oil   Freshly ground black pepper   Beaten egg to glaze**

Set oven to 400°F or Mark 6. Sift flour into a bowl. Grate the butter into the flour, stirring occasionally to mix. Add 4-5 tablespoons cold water and mix to a dough. Knead lightly then chill in the refrigerator for 30 minutes. Roll out half the pastry and line a greased 9 inch loose bottomed tart tin. Cover with greaseproof paper and fill with baking beans. Bake blind in preheated oven for 15 minutes. Reduce oven temperature to 375°F or Mark 5. Put cream cheese, eggs, parsley in a food processor and blend well. Heat oil in a pan and cook onion until softened. Place Stilton, walnuts and onion in a bowl. Add cream cheese mixture and season with pepper, stirring well. Spoon into pastry case. Roll out remaining pastry ½ inch larger than the base. Brush base edges with egg, cover with lid and pinch edges together to seal. Brush with beaten egg to glaze and bake for 40 minutes.

Chicken Picnic Pie

*Marinated chicken strips are layered with sausagemeat
and topped with a pastry lid.*

**8 oz. shortcrust pastry chilled   Beaten egg for glazing
1½ lbs. boneless chicken cut into ½" strips
1 lb. pork sausagemeat   1 teaspoon mace   6 spring onions, chopped
Juice and rind of a lemon   1 teaspoon fresh thyme
1 tablespoon fresh sage   2 tablespoons double cream
Salt and ground black pepper**

Set oven to 400°F or Mark 6. Use half the pastry to line a greased round 8 inch diameter sloping sided pie dish. Marinate the chicken strips with the mace, seasoning and a little lemon juice. Mix the sausagemeat, spring onions, herbs, lemon rind and 2 tablespoon lemon juice together. Pour in the cream, mixing well. Put one third of this mixture in the pastry base, spread flat and cover with half the chicken. Add a second layer of sausagemeat, followed by the remaining chicken and finally the third layer of sausagemeat. Roll out the remaining pastry and cover the pie. Moisten and seal the edges well. Glaze with the beaten egg and bake for 30 minutes. Reduce the heat to 350°F or Mark 4 and cook for another 1¼ hours. Serves 6-8.

Salmon Cream Flan

*A creamy salmon filling decorated with overlapping slices
of cucumber makes an attractive dish for a buffet.*

6 oz. flour	**3 oz. butter**
Pinch of salt	**Cold water to mix**

FILLING:

1 x 7 oz. can red salmon	**¼ teaspoon anchovy essence**
2 eggs	**3 spring onions, chopped finely**
¼ cucumber peeled and diced	**Salt and pepper**
½ pint single cream	**Cucumber to garnish**

Set oven to 425°F or Mark 7. Sieve the flour & salt into a bowl. Rub in the butter until mixture resembles fine breadcrumbs. Slowly add sufficient cold water to make a rolling dough. Roll out and line a greased 8 inch flan tin. Cover base with greaseproof paper and baking beans and bake blind for 10-15 minutes. Meanwhile, flake the salmon in a bowl and beat in the eggs. Add the chopped cucumber, cream, anchovy essence, onion and season to taste. Remove the beans and paper from the pastry case and spoon in the salmon mixture. Reduce oven temperature to 325°F or Mark 3 and bake for 30-35 minutes until the filling has set. Garnish with slices of cucumber. Serves 4-6.

Lamb Pie

An old Welsh recipe, traditionally made with the first of the spring lamb.

1½ lb. neck of lamb	3 to 4 carrots, peeled and sliced
1 onion, peeled and chopped	1 dessertspoon fresh chopped parsley
2 sprigs parsley	8 oz. prepared shortcrust pastry
Salt and black pepper	A little beaten egg to glaze

Remove the meat from the bone and cut into dice. Put the bones in a saucepan with the onion, parsley sprigs and seasoning, cover with water, boil for 1 to 1½ hours, then strain and reserve the liquid. Set oven to 350°F or Mark 4. Line the base of a 1½ to 2 pint pie dish with the carrots, cover with the diced lamb, then sprinkle over the parsley and seasoning. Roll out the pastry on a lightly floured surface and use to cover the pie, sealing the edges well and trimming neatly. Make a steam hole in the centre of the pie, brush with beaten egg and cook for 1¾ to 2 hours or until golden brown. Reheat the strained stock and, using a funnel, pour into the pie through the steam hole just before serving. Serve with mashed potatoes and green peas. Serves 4 to 6.

Tomato and Basil Quiche

A favourite traditional brunch, quiche is usually served at room temperature or chilled.

**6 oz. shortcrust pastry   1 oz. butter   1 onion, sliced thinly
5 large tomatoes, skinned and sliced thinly   3 eggs
¼ pint single cream   2 oz. grated Cheddar cheese
2 tablespoons chopped fresh basil   Salt and pepper**

Set oven to 400°F or Mark 6. Roll out pastry and use to line a 9 inch flan case. Melt the butter in a frying pan, add the onion and fry for 5 minutes. Remove from pan and spread over bottom of flan case. Arrange the tomatoes over the onions. Combine the cream, eggs and cheese, stir in the basil, and season to taste. Pour mixture over the tomatoes, place dish on a baking sheet and bake for 40 minutes until the filling is firm and golden brown. Serves 4-6.

Gammon and Apricot Pie

The combination of gammon or ham with apricots dates back at least to Elizabethan days. This recipe is from Buckinghamshire.

4 gammon steaks, approx. 1 inch thick	**Black pepper**
1 to 1½ oz. butter	**½ oz. sultanas**
5 oz. dried apricots (the no-soak type are ideal)	**½ pint pork stock**
	1 to 1½ lb. potatoes, peeled and parboiled, then cut into slices

Set oven to 350°F or Mark 4. Fry the gammon lightly on both sides in half the butter. Arrange in a 1½ to 2 pint pie dish and cover with the apricots. Season lightly with pepper, then sprinkle over the sultanas. Pour on the stock and cover the filling with overlapping layers of potatoes. Melt the remaining butter and brush over the potatoes. Cover the pie with a piece of kitchen foil and bake for 1 hour then remove the foil and bake for a further 20 to 30 minutes to brown the potatoes. Serve with carrots and peas. Serves 4.

Leek and Mushroom Tart

Leeks are an excellent source of vitamin C, iron and fibre. Choose small or medium size leeks, less than an inch diameter with fresh green leaf tops.

8 inch, baked shortcrust pastry flan case   2 medium leeks
1 oz. butter   4 oz. sliced mushrooms   Salt and pepper
2 eggs   5 fl. oz. milk   6 oz. Edam cheese, grated

Set oven to 350°F or Mark 4. Trim leeks and slice into ½ inch rings, washing well. Heat the butter in a pan, add the leeks, cover and cook for 10 minutes. Add the mushrooms and seasoning and cook for 5 minutes. Use a slotted spoon to remove the vegetables and place them in the flan case. Beat the eggs and milk in a bowl and season well. Add the cheese and sprinkle over the vegetables. Bake for 30 minutes until set and golden brown. Serves 4.

Lamb and Apple Pie

*A tasty meal served with creamed potatoes and carrots, this dish
is called Squab Pie in the Cotswolds.*

**8 oz. shortcrust pastry
12 small best-end-of-neck lamb cutlets
1 large cooking apple, peeled, cored and sliced
2 onions, peeled and sliced   Salt and black pepper
½ teaspoon ground nutmeg   ¼ pint lamb stock**

Set oven to 400°F or Mark 6. Place half the lamb in a 1½ to 2 pint pie dish and layer half the apple and onion slices on top. Sprinkle with seasoning and nutmeg, then place the remainder of the lamb and the apple and onion slices on top. Pour on the stock. Roll out the pastry on a lightly floured surface and cover the pie, trimming the edges neatly and sealing well. Use trimmings for decoration and make a small 'steam hole' in the centre of the lid. Brush with milk or beaten egg to glaze. Bake for 20 minutes, then lower the oven temperature to 350°F or Mark 4 and cook for a further 1 to 1¼ hours. Serves 4.

Lenten Pie

If desired this can be served as a flan by halving the pastry requirement and omitting the pastry lid.

1 lb. prepared shortcrust pastry   1 oz. butter   1 onion, peeled and chopped
1 clove garlic, peeled and crushed
2 to 3 bunches of watercress, trimmed, rinsed, well-drained and chopped
3 eggs, beaten   ¼ pint milk   ¼ pint single cream
2 to 3 tablespoons fresh, chopped herbs parsley, chives, thyme, etc.
Salt and black pepper   ¼ teaspoon grated nutmeg
1 heaped tablespoon grated cheese (if desired)

Set oven to 375°F or Mark 5. Grease a 9 inch flan dish. Roll out the pastry on a lightly floured surface and use half to line the flan dish, trimming the edges neatly. Bake blind for 15 to 20 minutes. Melt the butter in a saucepan and cook the onion and garlic until soft then add the watercress and cook for 1 to 2 minutes, stirring once or twice. Beat the eggs and milk together, then stir in the cream, herbs, seasoning and nutmeg. Add the watercress mixture and combine well. Turn into the flan dish and sprinkle over the grated cheese, if desired. Top with the remaining pastry, sealing the edges well and trimming neatly. Make a small steam hole in the centre and glaze with a little milk or beaten egg. Bake for about 30 minutes until the filling is set and the pastry top golden. Serve hot or cold. Serves 4 to 6.

Steak and Oyster Pie

The flavour of this pie will be improved if the meat filling is cooked the day before.

1 tablespoon cooking oil   1 oz butter
1½ lb. braising steak, cut into 1 inch cubes
1 medium onion, peeled and diced
2 tablespoons plain flour   ½ pint beef stock   ¼ pint red wine
1 tablespoon tomato purée   ½ teaspoon dried mixed herbs
1 small tin smoked oysters (drained)   8 oz. puff pastry

Set oven to 325°F or Mark 3. Heat the oil in a large frying pan, add the butter and fry the beef in small batches until browned, and transfer to a casserole dish. Fry the onion gently until soft and lightly browned. Stir in the flour and cook for 2 to 3 minutes. Remove from the heat and add the stock, wine, tomato purée and herbs. Return to the heat and, stirring, bring to the boil. Pour over the meat, cover and cook in the oven for 1½ hours. Stir in the oysters and cook for a further 30 minutes. Next, transfer the meat to a 3 pint pie dish and insert a pie funnel in the centre. Roll out the pastry on a lightly floured surface and use to cover the pie dish. Trim and decorate. Increase oven to 425°F or Mark 7. When hot, cook the pie for 25 minutes then reduce oven to 350°F or Mark 4 and cook for a further 15 minutes. Serves 4 to 6.

Caramelised Onion Tart

Caramelising onions gives them a sweeter flavour.
Serve with a simple salad for a light lunch or supper.

8 oz. shortcrust pastry made with wholemeal flour
2 tablespoons olive oil
1 lb. large red onions peeled and sliced thinly
Salt and pepper   1 teaspoon balsamic vinegar
5 fl. oz. milk   3 eggs   5 fl. oz. double cream
Pinch of freshly grated nutmeg
6 oz. grated Gruyère cheese

Set oven to 400°F or Mark 6. Roll out pastry and line a greased 8 inch flan tin. Heat oil in a frying pan, add onions, cover, and cook until soft, stirring frequently. Season with salt and pepper to taste, reduce the heat and cook until onions are very soft, and golden brown (takes 30-40 minutes) stirring occasionally. Add balsamic vinegar and cook for a further 10 minutes until onions are well caramelised. Remove from heat and set aside to cool. Sprinkle half the cheese in the pastry case, cover with onions and top with rest of cheese. Whisk milk, cream and eggs together, season with nutmeg, salt and pepper. Pour over onions and cheese and bake for 35-40 minutes until set. Stand for 5-10 minutes before serving. Serves 6.

Sausage Pie

This pie made with sausage meat is very adaptable. It can be eaten hot or cold and is a very useful addition to the picnic hamper.

8 oz. shortcrust pastry	1 level teaspoon chopped parsley
¾ lb. pork sausage meat	2 tablespoons chicken stock
1 small onion, finely chopped	1 small beaten egg
1 level teaspoon chopped chives	Salt and black pepper

Set oven to 375°F or Mark 5. Grease an 8 inch ovenproof pie dish. Roll out the pastry on a floured surface and use two-thirds to line the pie dish. In a bowl, and using only half the quantity of beaten egg, mix together all the ingredients very well with a fork. Place the mixture in the pie dish and level off. Top with a pastry lid and trim and flute the edges with the back of a knife; make a steam hole in the centre. Glaze the pastry with the remaining beaten egg. Bake for 15 minutes then reduce oven to 325°F or Mark 3 and continue baking for 30 to 45 minutes until the pie is cooked through. Serve hot with vegetables or cold with salad. Serves 4 to 6.

Smoked Haddock and Cheese Flan

A tasty creamy flan which can also be made with milk instead of cream, herrings or kippers and or dry grated cheese instead of the cottage cheese for a more thrifty version.

8 oz. smoked haddock	8 inch baked pastry flan case
5 fl. oz. water	2 eggs, beaten
Juice of ½ lemon	6 tablespoons single cream
1 oz. butter	4 oz. cottage cheese
1 onion, chopped finely	1 tablespoon chopped fresh parsley
2 oz. button mushrooms, chopped	Salt and pepper

Set oven to 375°F or Mark 5. Place haddock, water and half the lemon juice in a pan and poach fish. Drain, remove skin and bones and flake the flesh. Melt the butter in a pan, add onion and cook for 2 minutes then add chopped mushrooms and cook for a further 4 minutes. Combine the fish and vegetables and spoon over base of pastry case. Add the cream, cheese lemon juice and parsley to the beaten eggs. Season to taste. Pour into pastry case and bake in the preheated oven for 30-35 minutes until set and browned. Serves 4-6.

Roman Pie

A filling pie, packed with meat, pasta and vegetables, topped with puff pastry.

1 lb. puff pastry	1 tablespoon butter
1 rabbit or small chicken (jointed)	1 pint chicken or vegetable stock
1 medium sized onion	Salt and pepper
1 medium sized leek	2 oz. cooked macaroni
1 medium sized carrot	2 oz. grated cheese
2 mushrooms	3 tablespoons single cream

Set oven to 350°F or Mark 4. Soften the onion in the butter in a saucepan and add the other vegetables. Place in a greased casserole and add the rabbit or chicken joints. Season and pour on the stock. Cover the dish and cook for approximately 1 hour or until tender. Remove from oven and leave to cool. Flake the meat from the bones. Reset the oven to 425°F or Mark 7. Roll out the pastry and line an 8 inch pie dish with part of it. Place half of the meat, vegetables, macaroni and cheese in layers in the dish, then repeat with the remaining ingredients. Pour on the liquid from the casserole with the cream and cover with a pastry lid. Make a hole in the centre of the lid. Brush with a little milk. Bake for ½ hour, lower the oven temperature to 375°F or Mark 5 and cook for a further ½ hour. Serves 4 to 5.

Vegetable Pie

In this vegetarian pie the fish can be omitted, if preferred, and extra cheese added.

4 medium potatoes	**1 leek, sliced**
2 medium carrots or other vegetables	**2 peppers (any colour) de-seeded**
e.g. parsnip, as available	**and chopped**
1 tablespoon olive oil	**4 tomatoes, quartered or sliced**
1 oz. butter	**(or 8 cherry tomatoes)**
1 large or 3 small onions, chopped	**200 g can of tuna in oil, drained**
2 cloves of garlic, crushed	**2-3 oz. of hard cheese, grated**

Boil the potatoes in salted water and mash them. If using carrots or other root vegetables, parboil them for about 15 minutes before including with the other vegetables in the frying pan. Melt the oil and butter in a frying pan and fry the onions, garlic, leek, peppers and whatever other vegetables are being used and lastly the tomatoes. When cooked, put the vegetable mixture in the bottom of a flameproof dish. Mix together the mashed potato and tuna and use to cover the vegetables. Sprinkle over the grated cheese, put under a hot grill and brown. Serves 4.

Chopped fried bacon (4 rashers) or other cooked fish (½ lb.) could be mixed with the mashed potato instead of the tuna if desired. If the fish or bacon are omitted from the mashed potatoes use 2 oz. more cheese in the mixture.

Raised Veal and Ham Pie

*The pastry is mixed with boiling water, making a pliable dough which
can be moulded into a raised pie that holds its shape.*

PASTRY:

**1 lb. plain flour   2 teaspoons salt   4 oz. lard   9 fl. oz. water   ¾ lb. diced pie veal
4 oz. chopped ham   1 tablespoon chopped parsley   Grated rind and juice of a lemon
Salt and pepper   A little water   1 hard boiled egg   Beaten egg to glaze
Jelly stock (2 tablespoons gelatine dissolved in ½ pint chicken stock)**

Set oven to 425°F or Mark 7. Mix flour and salt and make a well in the centre.
Melt lard in water, boil and pour into well. Beat quickly with a wooden spoon
to a soft dough. Knead until smooth. Cover with a damp teatowel and leave to
rest for 30 minutes. Roll out ⅔ of pastry into an 11x10 inch oval. Grease a
round cake tin, drape pastry over rolling pin and unroll over tin. (Keep
remaining pastry covered with a damp cloth.) Press into tin and raise to ¼ inch
above the rim. Mix veal, ham parsley, lemon rind and juice, season to taste and
add a little water to moisten. Half fill pastry case with meat mixture, place egg
in the centre, add remaining meat and cover with rest of pastry rolled to fit the
top. Pinch edges together and flute. Glaze with beaten egg combined with a
little water. Make a small hole in centre with a sharp knife. Tie a band of
greaseproof paper around pie. Cook for 15-20 minutes then reduce heat to
350°F or Mark 4 and cook for a further 1½ hours until meat is tender. When
cold, fill pie with jelly stock. Leave to set.   *Twenty-Seven*

Cheese Crust Vegetable Pie

Tasty garden vegetables wrapped in a savoury cheese pastry.

CHEESE PASTRY:

**6 oz. flour   ½ teaspoon salt   ½ teaspoon dried mustard powder   4 oz. butter
3 oz. Cheddar cheese, finely grated   Water   Vegetable filling
3 medium carrots, peeled and diced   6 oz. corn kernels   2 medium onions, finely diced
1 clove garlic, crushed   2 oz. fresh peas   ½ medium swede, peeled and diced**

SAUCE:

**1½ oz. flour   1½ oz. margarine   ¾ pint of milk
Salt and pepper   Dried mixed herbs to taste**

Prepare the pastry by the traditional rubbing-in method or in a food processor. Place in the refrigerator to rest. Set oven to 375°F or Mark 5. Place all the vegetables, except the peas, in a large saucepan with 2–3 tablespoons of water, cover and cook gently until tender. Stir in the peas. Make the sauce by melting the margarine, adding the flour and cooking for 2–3 minutes. Remove from the heat and gradually add the milk, beating well between each addition. Return to the heat and, stirring continuously, bring to the boil. Add the vegetables to the sauce with the mixed herbs and season well. Put into a pie dish and immediately cover with the cheese pastry. Bake until the pastry is golden in colour; 35 minutes approximately. The vegetables in this pie can be varied according to what is in season.

Country Chicken Pie

This pie can be made in advance and frozen uncooked.

1 oz. butter	Juice of ½ lemon
1 oz. flour	10 oz. cooked chicken, diced
10 fl. oz. milk	4 oz. cooked ham or bacon, diced
Salt and pepper	3 carrots, cooked and chopped

8 oz. frozen puff pastry, thawed

Set oven to 425°F or Mark 7. Melt butter in a pan and add flour. Stir well and cook for 1 minute. Slowly add the milk, stirring continuously. Bring to the boil and simmer for 2 minutes, stirring well. Add remaining ingredients and mix thoroughly. Spoon into an oven proof pie dish and roll out pastry to cover. Decorate the top of the pie with the trimmings. Bake in the oven for 30 minutes, reducing the heat to 350°F or Mark 4 after 15 minutes. Serves 4.

Ratatouille Tart

Be careful not to overcook the vegetables and drain off any excess liquid
before adding eggs and transferring to pastry case.

2 tablespoons olive oil   1 green pepper, finely sliced
1 onion, peeled and chopped   1 garlic clove, crushed
1 lb. courgettes, washed and thinly sliced
4 tomatoes peeled, de-seeded and chopped
1 teaspoon sugar   3 beaten eggs
2 oz. Cheddar cheese, grated   Salt and pepper
8 inch pastry flan case

Set oven to 375°F or Mark 5. Heat the oil in a frying pan, add the green pepper and onion and cook gently to soften. Add the garlic, tomatoes, courgettes, sugar and season to taste. Cover and simmer gently for 30 minutes until vegetables are softened. Remove from heat and allow to cool. Gently stir in the beaten eggs and spoon into the pastry case. Sprinkle the top with the cheese. Bake in the preheated oven for 40 minutes. Do not overcook the vegetables. Drain off any excess liquid before adding eggs and transferring to pastry case. Serves 4-6.

Corned Beef Pie

Corned beef is traditionally served on Easter Sunday in Ireland.
It is also served on St. Patrick's Day.

2 x 12 oz. cans of corned beef   2 onions, chopped   1 tablespoon oil
Salt and pepper   1 teaspoon Tabasco sauce   1 egg, beaten
3 cooked carrots, diced   4 oz. cooked frozen peas
8 oz. shortcrust pastry   1 egg for glazing   Parsley to decorate

Set oven to 425°F or Mark 7. Mash corned beef and put into a bowl. Heat oil in a frying pan, add onions and cook until soft. Remove from heat and add to corned beef. Season well and add Tabasco sauce, beaten egg and vegetables. Divide pastry in half and roll out one piece and use to line an 8 inch pie plate. Spoon filling into case and cover with remaining pastry rolled to size. Decorate with trimmings and glaze with the beaten egg. Bake in oven for 25-30 minutes then reduce temperature to 350°F or Mark 4 for a further 20 minutes. Garnish with parsley. Serves 6.

Crispy Spinach Pie

*Once cooked the filo pastry remains crisp, making this a dish
suitable to be eaten cold for a picnic.*

**2 lb. fresh spinach, chopped   2 tablespoons vegetable oil
1 garlic clove, crushed   2 onions, sliced thinly   2 oz. melted butter
4 tablespoons chopped fresh parsley   8 oz. feta cheese
4 eggs   ½ teaspoon grated nutmeg   Ground black pepper   1 lb. filo pastry**

Set oven to 375°F or Mark 5. Wash and drain spinach. In a large frying pan, heat the oil and add onions and garlic and fry for 5 minutes. Add the spinach, cover and allow to cook gently for 8 minutes. Remove lid, turn up the heat and stir until all the liquid has evaporated. Remove from the heat, stir in the parsley and leave to cool. Use a fork to mash the feta cheese and beat in the eggs. Combine with the spinach and nutmeg and season well. Grease a Swiss roll tin with melted butter and layer half the sheets of filo pastry into it, ensuring that each sheet is brushed with melted butter. Spread the filling on top of the pastry sheets and cover with the remaining filo pastry brushing with melted butter as before. Cover top layer with more melted butter and cook for 1 hour until crispy and browned. Serve warm or cold with a green or Greek salad. Serves 8.

Bacon and Egg Pie

A shallow pastry-covered tart with sliced sausages in the filling.
A simple and tasty supper dish.

1 lb. shortcrust pastry	2 eggs, beaten
2 sausages	1 tablespoon chopped fresh parsley
3 rashers bacon, de-rinded	Salt and pepper

Set oven to 400°F or Mark 6. Grease an 8-inch sponge tin. Roll out half the pastry on a floured surface and use to line the tin. Cut up the sausages and bacon (either back or streaky) into pieces and arrange over the pastry case. Pour over the beaten eggs. Sprinkle over the chopped parsley and season to taste. Roll out the remaining pastry, cover the pie, seal the edge firmly and make a steam hole. Bake for about 45 minutes until golden brown. Serve cold with a green salad. Serves 3 to 4.

Stilton Tart

This distinctive English cheese with its creamy texture and tangy flavour combines well with the peppery flavour of the watercress.

1 lb. shortcrust pastry   1 oz. unsalted butter
A bunch of spring onions, trimmed and chopped into 2 inch lengths
4 oz. frozen peas   4 medium eggs, beaten   5 fl. oz. single cream
A bunch of watercress, trimmed and roughly chopped
5 oz. Stilton, cut into ¼ inch cubes   Salt and pepper
12 cherry tomatoes, halved

Set oven to 400°F or Mark 6. Line a 10 inch greased flan tin with the pastry. Prick the base with a fork, cover with greaseproof paper and baking beans and bake blind for 10 minutes. Remove paper and beans and return pastry case to oven for 5-10 minutes until cooked and crisp. Remove from oven and allow to cool slightly. Lower oven temperature to 350°F or Mark 4. Melt butter in a pan, add onions and peas, stirring over low heat for 30 seconds. Cover and cook for 3 4 minutes until softened. Remove from heat and set aside to cool. Meanwhile, in a bowl, combine the cream, eggs, half of the watercress and half of the Stilton. Season, add onions and peas, stirring well. Spoon into pastry case and distribute tomato halves evenly across the top. Sprinkle rest of Stilton over the top and cook for 30-35 minutes until set and browned. Serve warm or cold garnished with remaining watercress. Serves 4.

Country Potato Topped Pie

*Seal straight from the oven for a complete family meal of
meat and vegetables covered with creamy mash.*

**1½ lb. potatoes, peeled   1 oz. butter   3 tablespoons milk
Salt and pepper   1 oz. lard   ¼ lb. onion, peeled and chopped
1 lb. lean minced beef   ¼ lb. bacon rashers, rind removed and chopped
1 tablespoon cornflour   ¼ pint beef stock   Large tin chopped tomatoes
4 oz. frozen peas**

Set oven to 400°F or Mark 6. Boil potatoes in salted water until soft, drain and
mash with the butter and milk until creamy. Season to taste. Heat the lard in a
frying pan and fry onion until soft and browned. Add the mince and bacon
and fry over gentle heat, stirring to break up any lumps for 5 minutes. Add
seasoning, cornflour and stir well. Pour in the stock, bring to the boil, stirring
constantly, reduce heat and simmer for 5 minutes. Spoon half the mince
mixture into a 2½ pint ovenproof dish, cover with the tomatoes, peas, and then
the rest of the mince. Pipe the creamed potato over the top and bake in the
oven for 40 minutes until the top is nicely browned. Serves 4.

Sardine and Tomato Flan

*Arrange the anchovies radiating out from the centre, interspersed
with the olives for a decorative effect.*

9 inch shortcrust pastry flan case
1 onion, peeled and blanched in boiling water for 5 minutes
1 x 10 oz. can of sardines, drained   3 thinly sliced tomatoes
6 pitted black olives   6 anchovy fillets   3 medium eggs
6 fl. oz. single cream   Salt and pepper

Set oven to 400°F or Mark 6. Chop blanched onion and cover bottom of flan
case with them. Lay the tomatoes and sardines over the onion and decorate
with anchovies and olives. Combine the eggs and cream and season to taste.
Carefully pour over flan filling. Bake in oven for 40 minutes until set and
browned. Serve hot or cold. Serves 4-6.

Pork and Chestnut Pie

Light and tasty, this pie combines the traditional flavours of Christmas.

12 oz. flour   4 oz. butter   2 oz. lard
½ teaspoon salt   3 fl. oz. water

FILLING:
12 oz. pork fillet, chopped roughly
12 oz. tinned whole chestnuts, chopped roughly
12 oz. cranberries   1 small onion, finely chopped
1 tablespoon cooking oil   1 teaspoon chopped thyme
1 teaspoon chopped sage   3 eggs, beaten   Salt and pepper

In a bowl, rub the fats into the flour and stir in the salt. Mix to a dough with the cold water, wrap in cling film and chill for 1 hour. Set oven to 400°F or Mark 6. Heat the oil in a pan and cook the onions until soft but not browned. Place the pork and chestnuts in a large bowl and add the onion. Stir in the herbs and seasoning to taste and mix well. Beat 2 eggs and add to the bowl with the cranberries, stirring thoroughly to combine. Roll out two thirds of the pastry on a floured surface and line a loose based 9½ inch flan tin. Fill with the pork mixture, smoothing it out evenly. Roll out the rest of the pastry to make a lid, cover and seal the edges with water. Beat the remaining egg and brush over the pie to glaze. Bake for 40-50 minutes. Serve hot or cold.

"Preparing the Meal"

Savoury Chicken Tart

A useful picnic recipe or standby meal when pressed for time.
Cooked chicken left-overs may be added.

1 can condensed cream of chicken soup
2 eggs, beaten   Milk or water   1 large tomato, sliced
Salt and pepper   8 oz. shortcrust pastry

Set oven to 425°F or Mark 7. Roll out pastry and use to line a 7 inch flan dish. Cover the bottom of the flan with slices of tomato. Tip can of condensed soup into a measuring jug, add eggs and top up to ¾ pint with the milk or water. Season to taste with salt and freshly ground black pepper and pour carefully into pastry case. Bake for 15 minutes then reduce heat to 375°F or Mark 5 and bake until the filling is set and the pastry is crispy. Serve with sliced tomato and a green salad. Serves 6.

Turkey Pie

An easily made dish, rather like a cottage pie, which uses left-over cooked turkey. Useful after Christmas.

1 lb. cooked turkey, diced
1 small onion, peeled and chopped   2 oz. butter
4 oz. sweetcorn kernels (frozen or tinned)
1 tablespoon chopped parsley or chives   Black pepper
15 oz. tin condensed soup (choice optional)   1 tablespoon sherry
1½ lb. mashed potato beaten with 1 small egg

Set oven to 325°F or Mark 3. First peel the potatoes and cook in salted water to make the mash. Meanwhile, melt the butter in a pan and fry the onion for a few minutes to soften, but not brown. Stir in the diced turkey, sweetcorn and herbs and season with pepper. Gradually stir in the soup and sherry over a low heat and continue stirring until heated through. Transfer to an ovenproof dish. Mash the potatoes and beat in the egg. Top the dish with mashed potato and cook in the oven for 30 to 40 minutes until browned on top. Serve with green vegetables and chutney. Serves 4.

Gardener's Pie

Courgettes are the basis of this vegetable crumble,
which has cheese and mixed nuts in the topping.

3 tablespoons walnut oil   2 onions, peeled and sliced
3 cloves of garlic, peeled and crushed
2 lb. courgettes, washed, trimmed and cut into ½ inch slices
1 lb. tomatoes, skinned and chopped   2 tablespoons tomato purée
3 or 4 basil leaves, chopped   Salt and pepper

TOPPING:
3 oz. fresh brown breadcrumbs
2 oz. Cheddar cheese, grated
2 oz. chopped mixed nuts

Set oven to 350°F or Mark 4. Heat the oil in a large saucepan, add the onions and garlic and cook gently for 5 minutes. Add all the remaining ingredients, season and cook for a further 5 minutes. Turn into a 3 pint ovenproof dish. Topping: mix together the topping ingredients and sprinkle evenly over the vegetables. Cook in the oven for about 30 minutes. Serve hot with crusty bread. Serves 4.

Double Crust Pie

*A double crust pie is one made with both a bottom and a top crust
with a filling between them.*

**2 oz. sliced mushrooms   1 small onion, peeled and sliced
2 oz. cooking oil   1 teaspoon curry powder
1 lb. lean raw minced beef   5 fl. oz. beef gravy
Salt and pepper   7 oz. shortcrust pastry**

Set oven to 400°F or Mark 6. Heat cooking oil in a frying pan, add mushrooms
and onion and fry gently for about 5 minutes until just softened. Stir in the
curry powder and cook for a further 2-3 minutes. Add the mince and heat,
stirring well to break up any lumps. Stir in the gravy and season to taste.
Remove from heat. Roll out half the pastry and use to line a greased 8 inch pie
dish. Add the filling. Roll out the remaining pastry and cover the pie, sealing
the edges well. Trim the edges and scallop. Bake for 30 minutes until the pastry
has browned. Lower the temperature to 350°F or Mark 4 and cook for a
further 15-20 minutes. Serves 4-6.

Cheese, Tomato and Bacon Tart

Cheese tarts in various forms make versatile and satisfying dishes which taste as good eaten cold or hot. Smoked bacon would add to the flavour, if preferred.

8 oz. shortcrust pastry
6 oz. streaky bacon, cut into pieces
1 large onion, roughly chopped
1 clove garlic, crushed
Cooking oil

2 eggs, beaten
¼ pint milk
Freshly ground black pepper
2 oz. Cheddar cheese, grated
2 tomatoes, sliced into wheels

A sprinkling of oregano or basil

Set oven to 375°F or Mark 5. Butter a 9 inch flan dish. Roll out the pastry on a floured surface and line the dish. Trim the edge. Prick the pastry all over with a fork and bake blind for about 10 minutes. Meanwhile, heat a little oil in a frying pan and fry the bacon and onion together with the garlic until the bacon is cooked and the onion is soft but not brown. Arrange the bacon, onion and garlic over the pastry base. In a jug, mix the beaten eggs with the milk and some twists of pepper and stir in half of the grated cheese. Pour the mixture over the bacon and onion. Arrange the tomato wheels over the top and sprinkle over the remaining grated cheese with a little oregano or basil. Bake for about 25 minutes until the topping is set. Serves 4 to 6.

METRIC CONVERSIONS

The weights, measures and oven temperatures used in the preceding recipes can be easily converted to their metric equivalents. The conversions listed below are only approximate, having been rounded up or down as may be appropriate.

Weights

Avoirdupois	Metric
1 oz.	just under 30 grams
4 oz. (¼ lb.)	app. 115 grams
8 oz. (½ lb.)	app. 230 grams
1 lb.	454 grams

Liquid Measures

Imperial	Metric
1 tablespoon (liquid only)	20 millilitres
1 fl. oz.	app. 30 millilitres
1 gill (¼ pt.)	app. 145 millilitres
½ pt.	app. 285 millilitres
1 pt.	app. 570 millilitres
1 qt.	app. 1.140 litres

Oven Temperatures

	°Fahrenheit	Gas Mark	°Celsius
Slow	300	2	150
	325	3	170
Moderate	350	4	180
	375	5	190
	400	6	200
Hot	425	7	220
	450	8	230
	475	9	240

Flour as specified in these recipes refers to plain flour unless otherwise described.